The Musicians

A play

Patrick Marber

Samuel French—London
New York-Toronto-Hollywood

© Patrick Marber, 2003
© 2005 revised and rewritten by Patrick Marber

Rights of Performance by Amateurs are controlled by Samuel French Ltd, 52 Fitzroy Street, London W1T 5JR, and they, or their authorized agents, issue licences to amateurs on payment of a fee. **It is an infringement of the Copyright to give any performance or public reading of the play before the fee has been paid and the licence issued.**

The Royalty Fee indicated below is subject to contract and subject to variation at the sole discretion of Samuel French Ltd.

> Basic fee for each and every
> performance by amateurs   Code E
> in the British Isles

The Professional Rights in this play are controlled by Judy Daish Associates Ltd, 2 St Charles Place, London W10 6EG.

The publication of this play does not imply that it is necessarily available for performance by amateurs or professionals, either in the British Isles or Overseas. Amateurs and professionals considering a production are strongly advised in their own interests to apply to the appropriate agents for written consent before starting rehearsals or booking a theatre or hall.

ISBN 0 573 05253 0

The right of Patrick Marber to be identified as author
of this work has been asserted in accordance with
Section 77 of the Copyright, Designs and Patents Act 1988.

Please see page iv for further copyright information

THE MUSICIANS

First performed as part of the National Theatre Connections Festival of 2004.

It received its London première at the Cottesloe Theatre in a production by Castleford High School on 7th July, 2004.

NOTE

This Acting Edition of *The Musicians* is the sole authorized text of the play and as such Patrick Marber wishes it to be used for all productions. Previously published texts should not be used.

COPYRIGHT INFORMATION
(See also page ii)

This play is fully protected under the Copyright Laws of the British Commonwealth of Nations, the United States of America and all countries of the Berne and Universal Copyright Conventions.

All rights, including Stage, Motion Picture, Radio, Television, Public Reading, and Translation into Foreign Languages, are strictly reserved.

No part of this publication may lawfully be reproduced in ANY form or by any means — photocopying, typescript, recording (including video-recording), manuscript, electronic, mechanical, or otherwise — or be transmitted or stored in a retrieval system, without prior permission.

Licences are issued subject to the understanding that it shall be made clear in all advertising matter that the audience will witness an amateur performance; that the names of the authors of the plays shall be included on all announcements and on all programmes; and that the integrity of the authors' work will be preserved.

The Royalty Fee is subject to contract and subject to variation at the sole discretion of Samuel French Ltd.

In Theatres or Halls seating Four Hundred or more the fee will be subject to negotiation.

In Territories Overseas the fee quoted in this Acting Edition may not apply. A fee will be quoted on application to our local authorized agent, or if there is no such agent, on application to Samuel French Ltd, London.

VIDEO-RECORDING OF AMATEUR PRODUCTIONS

Please note that the copyright laws governing video-recording are extremely complex and that it should not be assumed that any play may be video-recorded for *whatever purpose* without first obtaining the permission of the appropriate agents. The fact that a play is published by Samuel French Ltd does not indicate that video rights are available or that Samuel French Ltd controls such rights.

CHARACTERS

Alex
Roland
Second Flute
Cello
Second Trumpet
First Violin
Viola
Double Bass
Second Horn
First Horn
Timpani
Oboe
Clarinet
First Trumpet
Bassoon
First Flute

Except where obvious the musicians can be male or female.

A larger company may perform the play with a greater number of speaking roles by, for example, judiciously allotting some of **Violin**'s lines to a new character called **Second Violin**, etc. Alternatively, the company could keep the roles as written and have a much larger orchestra, some of whom don't have speaking parts. They will still have plenty to do.

"Pinball Wizard" by Pete Townshend
© 1969 Fabulous Music Limited
Suite 2.07, Plaza 535, Kings Road,
London SW10 0SZ
International copyright secured.
All rights reserved. Used by permission.

A licence issued by Samuel French Ltd to perform this play does not include permission to use the Incidental music specified in this copy. Where the place of performance is already licensed by the PERFORMING RIGHT SOCIETY a return of the music used must be made to them. If the place of performance is not so licensed then application should be made to the PERFORMING RIGHT SOCIETY, 29-33 Berners Street, London W1T 4AB.

A separate and additional licence from PHONOGRAPHIC PERFORMANCES LTD, Ganton House, 1 Upper James Street, London W1R 3HG is needed whenever commercial recordings are used.

THE MUSICIANS

Scene 1

The stage of a concert hall somewhere in Moscow

Chairs arranged for an orchestra to play; there is a lectern and a table

A young man in overalls, Alex, ambles on from the wings with a broom and dustpan. He idles to C and peers out at the auditorium. Suddenly, he raises his broom as if it's a guitar

Alex (*in Russian*) Good evening, Moscow! (*He makes the sound of two thousand people applauding—their whoops and screams—he modestly acknowledges the applause. In Russian*) Thank you, thank you!

Fantasy over, he reaches into his pocket, turns on his Walkman and starts sweeping. He sings to himself as he works. He is Russian, but sings in English—though with a Russian accent. He is listening to "Pinball Wizard" by The Who. He knows the song well and starts humming the opening guitar riff and then goes into Pete Townshend-style gyrations when the big chords come in. Once the vocals start, the broom becomes his microphone

> (*Singing*) Ever since I was a young boy,
> I played the silver ball,
> From Soho down to Brighton,
> I must have played 'em all,

> But I ain't seen nothin' like him
> In any amusement hall,
> That deaf, dumb and blind kid
> Sure plays a mean pinball!

Guitar break. He mimes with the broom. When the vocals return he becomes the pinball wizard on his machine

> (*Singing*) He stands like a statue,
> Becomes part of the machine,
> Feelin' all the bumpers,
> Always playin' clean.
> Plays by intuition,
> The digit counters fall.
> That deaf, dumb and blind kid
> Sure plays a mean pinball!

Roland appears in the wings. He is seventeen years old, intense, dedicated—but not without humour. He carries a small, black leather case. He watches Alex, somewhat embarrassed to be witnessing this private display of insanity

> (*Singing*) He's a pinball wizard, there has to be a twist,
> A pinball wizard's got such a supple wrist.
> (*In a very high voice*) How do you think he does it?
> (*Response*) I don't know!
> (*Further response*) What makes him so good?

Alex is freaking out. A one-man concert with full imaginary lasers and dry ice. Roland coughs but Alex can't hear

> (*Singing*) Ain't got no distractions,
> Can't hear no buzzes and bells,
> Don't see no lights a-flashin',
> Plays by sense of smell ——

Scene 1

Roland strides on to the stage so Alex can see him

Hey! Sorry! Hallo!

Alex turns off the Walkman. Roland nods to him and carefully places his case on a table

"Pinball Wizard", The Who.

Roland gives him a "thumbs up" then surveys the stage and the auditorium

You like The Who?

Roland considers what will best prevent further conversation

Roland I have no opinion.
Alex OK, I get message, shut cake-hole. (*He resumes his sweeping but watches Roland with curiosity*) Are you in group?

Roland is lost in thought

Hey! Britishman, are you make music?
Roland What?
Alex Speak English?
Roland Sometimes.
Alex You play music, la la la.
Roland Oh, yes.
Alex I like music! Alex.
Roland Roland.

They shake hands

Alex You orchestra, yes? From UK.
Roland Correct.
Alex How is Queen?

Roland She was fine when I last spoke to her.
Alex That is joke?

Roland nods

> British jokes, I know all about. Very ho ho ho. (*He gestures to Roland's case*) What instrument you have in box? Don't tell me. I'm guessing… (*He goes up to the case and inspects it*) You have double bass. (*Beat*) That is Russian joke.

Roland And most excellent it was.
Alex *I* play guitar. (*He briefly demonstrates using his broom. Wistfully*) I don't have guitar really but can pretend…

Roland looks sympathetic

> I like all English music: The Who best, then also Beatles, Stones, Pistols, Davie Bowie, The Smith, Oasis, Radiohead. Who you like?

Roland Val Doonican.
Alex Who?
Roland Val Doonican. He's new, you should check him out.

Alex takes out a pen and starts to write on his hand

Alex I write down. Val…?
Roland V—A—L.
Alex (*thinking*) You take piss?
Roland Just a bit.
Alex English humour: take piss, right?
Roland It's our national sport.

Alex looks at the case again

Alex So you play little erm…? (*He mimes a flute*)
Roland Flute?

Alex nods

> No.

Scene 1

Alex Play what you play?
Roland I'm not playing anything today.
Alex You singer? *I* sing.
Roland No, I'm not a singer.
Alex What are you do?

Roland goes to the case, dramatically releases the catches and produces a conductor's baton

You wave stick?
Roland I'm the *conductor*!
Alex Duh, I *know*! Who you conduct, famous people?
Roland The Ridley Road School Orchestra.

Alex conceals his disappointment

Alex You are boss man?
Roland Well, kind of…
Alex Kind of what?
Roland Well, usually I play the cello, but I've been conducting a few rehearsals recently. That's what I've always wanted; to be a conductor. Our music teacher's given me this one-off opportunity. So, if it goes well, who knows…?
Alex This big break for you?
Roland Yeah.
Alex Big scary break, wake in middle of night in sweat and screaming fear, yes?
Roland You could say that.
Alex Where from school?
Roland Croydon. (*Or wherever the company performing the play are based*)
Alex I have been in Wolverhampton. You know? I live Wolverhampton six week. On exchange. I stay with family Henderson.
Roland Please don't ask me if I know them.

For Fred

Alex Do you know them?
Roland No!
Alex Ken and Valerie Henderson. They have daughter, Donna. (*Mournfully*) She love Rio Ferdinand, football player. She say he have good body, tall and slim.
Roland Have you finished your cleaning yet, your sweeping? I don't mean to be rude, it's just that I really need to prepare.
Alex OK, I get. I bugger off.
Roland The stage looks perfect.
Alex I been sweep all day for you.
Roland Thank you.

Alex starts to exit

By the way, where is everyone? The technicians, sound people, lights?
Alex All take break.
Roland What, tea break?
Alex Vodka break, take longer.
Roland (*worriedly*) They'll be back for the concert, tonight?

Beat

Alex Concert? I thought you just practise.

Roland starts to panic

Roland We're giving a concert *tonight*, right *here*!
Alex *Here??* No-one say nothing.
Roland It's for an invited audience of dignitaries and cultural luminaries.
Alex Huh?
Roland "The European Festival of Youth" — there are posters all over town!
Alex I not see poster.
Roland We're representing our country, it's *incredibly* important!

Scene 1

Alex No-one say about concert, you make wrong mistake?

Roland mops his brow, sweating with anxiety now

Roland No! Look, here's the leaflet, it's *tonight*!
Alex (*reading*) Oh my God, *tonight*?!
Roland Yes, tonight!
Alex But it's impossible tonight!
Roland It's a catastrophe!

Alex starts laughing

Alex I piss take! I take piss! They come back in half hour!
Roland (*relieved but angry*) Are you familiar with the word "bastard"?
Alex And you with the word "tight-ass"?
Roland That's *two* words.
Alex Yeah, but only *one* tight-ass.

Roland shrugs, acknowledging the truth

So you practise music now?
Roland Once the musicians arrive, we'll be *rehearsing*, yes.
Alex I stay watch? Please?

Roland looks wary

Please, I silent. I never see orchestra before.
Roland Really?
Alex Only TV, not living.
Roland (*correcting him*) Live.
Alex Living, live, same thing?
Roland Not exactly. Now please, no more talking.
Alex I can see orchestra?
Roland If you *really* want to, yes—but you must be quiet, we desperately need this time to practise.

Alex (*confidentially*) Orchestra shit, need practise?
Roland *All* orchestras need practice — *rehearsal*. Now, *please*!
Alex I zip. (*He mimes zipping his mouth shut*) Also zip other place of talking. (*He mimes zipping his arse shut. He takes a chair and goes and sits near the wings with his broom and dustpan*)

Roland takes up a position C and practises with his baton. He silently goes through the opening section of the music. Alex watches, fascinated, as Roland communes with the music. Eventually:

What is the meaning of "Pinball Wizard"?
Roland I don't know!
Alex Is he wizard who like to play pinball? Or is he very good pinball player so people call him wizard?
Roland The latter—the second one. Now, *please*. (*He starts conducting again*)

As he is getting into it:

Alex Where is Brighton?
Roland (*furiously*) On the South coast of England! (*He starts conducting again*)

Alex can't stop himself

Alex Last question: what like, please, Brighton?
Roland It's got a beach! Sad, middle-aged businessmen with dandruff take their equally sad menopausal secretaries there for dirty weekends.
Alex Huh?
Roland They go there to have sex!
Alex But not Pinball Wizard, he go there to play pinball only?
Roland So it seems.
Alex And there is amusement hall in Brighton, like in song?
Roland I believe there are many amusement halls in Brighton.
Alex I like go Brighton. Have sex, play pinball, meet wizard. Have sex with wizard, who knows!

Scene 1

Roland May your wish come true! Now I really *must* get on!
Alex But what is *meaning* of song?
Roland I DON'T KNOW! It's just a bloody song! It doesn't MEAN ANYTHING! There is no Pinball Wizard, he doesn't exist, he's like the Tooth Fairy or Father Christmas!
Alex (*very seriously*) There *is* Pinball Wizard, he exist.
Roland NO, THERE ISN'T! HE DOESN'T!
Alex YES, HE DOES!
Roland NO, HE DOES NOT!
Alex YES! TO ME, THERE IS PINBALL WIZARD!
Roland HE DOESN'T EXIST!
Alex I BELIEVE IN HIM!
Roland WELL, YIPPEE FOR YOU—YOU BLOODY MUSCOVITE MORON!
Alex OK, OK, no need get shitty shirty. Everyone in world hate British people. Wonder why.

Roland sighs, pinches his brow

Roland Oh, help me, Lord. I'm very sorry, er… *Alex*. Forgive me? If you really want to know what the *meaning* of "Pinball Wizard" is, in my opinion, it is this: the song is metaphorical—symbolic, yes?

Alex nods

The Pinball Wizard is deaf, dumb and blind. He is therefore wholly unsuitable for his chosen field of endeavour—i.e. pinball. And yet, against seemingly insurmountable odds, he succeeds to such an extent that he is anointed a "Pinball Wizard". The song is testament to that tedious but seductive cliché, "the triumph of the human spirit in adversity". Now will you please SHUT UP!

Alex takes in the information, satisfied

Alex Thank you.

Roland continues to go through the music as Alex vaguely sweeps in the wings. He will be quietly observing the unfolding action

After a while, thirty musicians (more is preferable, less is acceptable) approach from off stage. A rumble of voices and noise from all sides. Roland looks panic-stricken as the sound intensifies. He rushes for the safety of his lectern

The musicians enter, talking and shouting in high spirits. Some of them acknowledge Roland but most of them are too preoccupied to notice him. They wear winter coats and stamp the snow from their shoes. It's freezing outside. Entrance dialogue to be improvised. It lasts twenty seconds maximum. Roland shouts above the hubbub

Roland Members of the orchestra, welcome! Welcome! Quickly, please! Please take your seats!

The musicians do so, knowing exactly where to sit

During this the Second Flute — a very keen young girl — staggers in with Roland's score — a big, heavy book. She positions it on the lectern in front of him. Then she hovers in readiness

By now, the orchestra are seated

Second Flute Anything else, maestro?

Roland hands her his baton which she cleans with a special cloth. The Cellist observes her

Cello What a creep!
Second Flute (*to Cello*) What a loser! (*She goes to sit with her fellow flautists*)

The musicians are now all seated, facing Roland. He taps his baton and after a while they pipe down

Scene 1

Roland Is everyone all right?

General murmurs of assent until Second Trumpet stands up

Second Trumpet Yeah, we're all marvellous, 'cept for one tiny thing: where's our *instruments*?!
Roland Ah, yes, apparently there was a bit of a mix-up at the airport. Mr Carmichael is in a van collecting the instruments as we speak.
First Violin What mix-up?
Roland Something to do with the hauliers, no need to panic.
Cello Who's panicking?
Roland Sorry?
Cello You said "no need to panic", implying that we were panicking. Who's panicking? I don't see anyone panicking.
Roland My apologies, I meant in a manner of speaking.
Viola (*to Cello*) Stop having a go, arsehole.

Murmurs of agreement from fellow viola players

All the way from Gatwick to Moscow, whinge, whinge, whinge.
Cello I'm only making a point.
Viola Your point is pointless.
Roland Well, no harm done. Now, is everyone happy with their accommodation?
Double Bass My shower doesn't work.
Second Horn So what, he never had a wash in his life!
First Trumpet Only soap he knows is *Emmerdale*!
Double Bass Sod off!
First Horn We're whiffing you from here!
Timpani And here! It mings like a farm!
Roland Members of the orchestra! Please let's behave like the ensemble we are! Now, while we're waiting I thought we could use this time to discuss Tchaikovsky's Fourth Symphony.

Murmurs of dissent and mock yawning from the Brass section

Picture the scene: It's February Eighteen Seventy-eight, the first performance of the Fourth Symphony right here in Moscow—not literally *here*, though it is in fact perfectly possible that Tchaikovsky may have once stood on this very stage. He might have actually stood where I'm standing now… (*He can't speak, he stares at the floor, overcome by the enormity of the thought*)

After a pause conversation breaks out

Oboe My telly's bust.
Cello There's nothing to watch anyway, it's all in bloody Russian.
Viola See! Always moaning, always got the hump.
Clarinet What I don't get is Chekhov. In *Three Sisters*, they're all going "Ooo, if only we could get to Moscow". *Why??*

Murmurs of agreement

First Trumpet At breakfast, they gave me black bread. It wasn't burnt toast, it was black bread. What's that all about?

Vociferous agreement

Oboe You go outside, it's so cold your breath turns to snow. It like goes solid coming out your mouth.
Bassoon Snow's not solid.
Oboe What is it, then? It ain't liquid or gas, so it's gotta be solid. There aren't any other forms of matter—unless you've invented one, Einstein.
Bassoon For your information, snow is a liquid.
Timpani Only when you piss on it!
Roland As I was saying, it's Eighteen Seventy-eight, Tchaikovsky's in *despair*; his marriage is a disaster, he's attempted suicide and guess what, he doesn't even attend his own première! He's written this magnificent masterpiece and he's too distraught to hear it … (*Once more he can't continue, too moved to speak*)
Second Horn Anyone seen those birds in the hotel lobby last night? I reckon they were prozzers.
Viola Did they talk to *you*?

Scene 1

Second Horn (*proudly*) Yeah!
Viola They must've been!
Second Trumpet Wonder how much they charge?
First Flute For *you*—about a billion roubles.
Timpani What's that then, ten p?
Roland Members of the orchestra! I must insist——
First Flute Anyone see those blokes with the big 'taches?
Viola Yeah, and the leather car coats—bet they were Mafia!
First Flute I wouldn't mind a bit of that!
Viola Yeah, you could end up owning a football club!
First Flute No, I'd make them buy me a castle like that Dr Zhivago.
Bassoon You what? He lived in a shack in the middle of nowhere!
First Flute Only at the end, not at the beginning *before* the Revolution.
Roland Can we please——
First Trumpet Anyone see that beggar?
First Horn What, the one passed out on the pavement?
First Trumpet D'you see all his snot and dribble had gone hard? If you gave him a little flick his whole head would shatter. It's sad really.
Second Trumpet When are the bloody instruments coming?
Clarinet Where's my clarinet?
First Violin Where's my violin?
Cello I want my cello!
Bassoon Where's my bassoon?
Second Trumpet Who's got my trumpet?
First Horn I want my horn!

Suddenly the whole orchestra stand and demand their instruments, like a many-headed beast. Pandemonium

Roland SOON! SOON! SOON! The instruments will be here soon, *please* be patient! (*Beat*) Now, please, let's discuss the music we're going to perform tonight.
First Violin *Murder* more like.
Roland I'm sorry?
First Violin You heard.

Roland Well, if we all adopt that kind of attitude we probably *will* murder it. So let's be positive.

First Violin Positive?! We spend so much time quarrelling and bickering and, quite frankly, listening to complete and utter garbage from "certain persons", that we never actually get any proper rehearsal time. We need to practise, practise, practise!

A few sarcastic "oohs" from the "certain persons"

Roland Actually, it's a fair point. Can I urge you all—just for today—to put aside your personal grievances and really commit yourselves to the music, just this once?

Clarinet I mean, how on earth did we ever *get* this booking? We're an absolute shambles.

Oboe It's obvious, there must've been a cancellation——

Second Horn And Carmichael wangled us in!

First Trumpet I bet he's taking a cut!

Second Trumpet And he's nicked our instruments!

First Horn He's pawning the lot in Vladivostock!

The Brass section start singing, softly at first and then getting louder as others begin to join in

Brass Section We're shit and we know we are, we're shit and we know we are!

Woodwind We're shit and we know we are!

Strings We're shit and we know we are!

The entire orchestra are now at full volume, all pointing in unison at the beleaguered, cowering Roland

All WE'RE SHIT AND WE KNOW WE ARE! WE'RE SHIT AND WE KNOW WE ARE!

Second Flute leaps up, screams with frustration

Second Flute STOP IT! STOP IT! STOP IT!

Scene 1

The singing fades away

(*With great passion*) You're all horrible! Horrible, nasty, mean and unfair. *You* might be here for a jolly old piss-up at the British taxpayer's expense but *Roland*'s here because he *lives* for music! This is supposed to be the greatest night of his life! Why can't you give him a chance? Why can't you behave like human beings instead of — of spoilt animals! There are people in Russia who would kill for the privileges we have, they *dream* of playing in an orchestra with proper instruments. You don't deserve Roland, he's too good for the whole mouldy lot of you!

Deathly silence. Second Flute sits down. Roland puts his head in his hands. He is, perhaps, the most embarrassed of them all

Roland (*softly, to Second Flute*) Thank you.

She nods, unashamed

Timpani (*murmuring*) We're still shit.

Others hush him up. Double Bass puts his hand up

Roland Yes?
Double Bass 'Scuse me, but erm… (*He whispers*) Who's *he*? (*He points to Alex*)

As one, in perfect unison, the orchestra turn to look at Alex

Roland Oh, this is Alex.

Alex waves, shyly, vaguely raises his broom

He was sweeping up when I arrived. He's never seen an orchestra before, he asked me if he could watch us rehearse. I hoped you wouldn't mind…

Silence. They are all ashamed of themselves

Alex (*amiably*) Hallo, British orchestra!

Chastened murmurs of "Hi", "How ya doing?", "Hallo", etc. Clarinet stands up, mortified

Clarinet May I officially apologize for our wholly unreasonable criticisms of your beautiful city.

Others murmur similar apologies. Second Flute is triumphant

Second Flute Well, it's a bit late now!
Oboe Better late than never.
Second Flute No, better to have never been so horribly rude!
Cello Why don't you button it for once in your life!
Viola (*to Cello*) Leave her alone, you big bully!
Second Flute (*to Viola*) Thank you, but I'm perfectly capable of defending myself against the rabble!

A row breaks out between the woodwind and strings. Roland's mobile rings. He shushes them to receive the call

Roland (*into the phone*) Mr Carmichael! (*He crouches at the front of the stage, finger in his ear*)

The orchestra strains to earwig the conversation

Yes, yes, all fine. Just in the middle of a fascinating debate about… Excuse me…? (*He listens*) Right. … When? (*He listens*) I *see*. … *Right*. … Yes. I will. (*He rings off. He is ashen*)

Everyone looks at him. Without warning he lets out a huge wail— a primal scream of incredible and surprising volume

AAAAAAAAGGGGGGHHHHHHH!!!

Scene 1

The entire orchestra shrink back as one—in fear and astonishment

You bastards! You shitting bloody bastards! Russian customs have impounded all your instruments! You're giving the most important concert of your lives in two hours time and you've got no instruments, you stupid, stupid bastards!

Consternation and panic break out in the orchestra

Do you want to know *why*?
All Yes!
Roland Well, *one* of you knows, don't you?
All No??

The entire orchestra turn to him

A Russian sniffer dog found a *spliff* hidden in one of the instruments!

Gasps and shock. Everyone looks at everyone accusingly, improvised protests of innocence and denial ring out

Cello Well, it wasn't me!
Viola We *know* that! You wouldn't know what a joint looks like!
Cello Oh, and I suppose you think it's cool to take drugs?
Viola In moderation, yes.
Oboe Who was it, Roland?
Second Trumpet Yeah, I'll kill him!
Clarinet It might be a *her*.

Clarinet glares at Viola

Viola Wasn't bloody *me*!
Double Bass Yeah, she only does crack!

Second Flute begins to emit a high-pitched wail. A strange, sad, sonic scream through her nose. All eyes gradually turn to her

Second Horn No!
Second Trumpet No way!
Oboe It's impossible!
Bassoon Still waters run deep...
First Flute Leave her alone, it wasn't her!
Second Flute It was! It was! It was *me*! (*She rushes for the exit*) I'm going to kill myself!

Various musicians prevent her leaving

Roland Why, *why*?
Second Flute I did it for *you*. It was for *you*!
Roland *Me??* I don't even smoke!
Second Flute But you get so anxious before a concert, I've seen you pacing around backstage, wearing a sad little strip in the carpet. And that's when you're only going to *play*. Now you're *conducting* I was scared you'd die of nerves. I thought a few quick puffs might relax you. I stole it from my sister. (*She sobs*) I didn't think anyone would check a flute.

Roland crumples into a chair, head in hands. Everyone else is in shock

Is Mr Carmichael going to expel me from the orchestra? He will, I know he will, my life is over!
Roland You're one of the top two flautists in Croydon. (*Or wherever*) No-one's kicking you out.
Double Bass What are we going to do?

Everyone turns to Roland hoping he's got the answer

Roland No other option. We'll have to cancel.

They are devastated

First Violin Can't we borrow some instruments, from another orchestra?

Scene 1

Alex In situation like this, have to ask very important question: what would Pinball Wizard do?

Roland manages a slight smile. He stares at his score for a few moments then closes it

Roland I really wanted you to hear this.
Alex Tchaikovsky?
Roland Mmm. Shall I send you the CD?
Alex Or maybe we meet in Brighton and you give to me?
Roland It's a deal. (*He paces and stands where Tchaikovsky might have stood. He raises his face to the heavens*) Pyotr Il'yich... I only wanted to honour you. I'm sorry. (*To Alex*) The irony is that old Tchaikovsky was condemned to death by his own schoolmates.
Alex They kill him?
Roland There was this sort of committee and they kind of forced him to kill himself.
Alex Why?
Roland Oh, he'd been having an affair with the son of some posh bloke.
Alex Tchaikovsky is poof?
Roland Er ... yeah ...
Alex Hmm. My brother is poof.
Roland Right...
Alex Are *you* poof?
Roland (*embarrassed*) Erm... I haven't decided yet. You?
Alex I think maybe *everyone* is a bit of poof.

Pause. Roland sits in abject misery

Roland You were right. I'm not a conductor. I never will be. I'm just a schoolboy waving a stick.

Pause

Alex What is word? Describe this music you were to play?

Roland Oh, well, you're asking me to describe the indescribable.
Alex Please, if can.

Roland thinks for a while. He speaks softly, slowly formulating his thoughts

Roland Well, it's beautiful. Really beautiful… (*Beat*) It's joy. And passion. And hope and despair … it's *life*. It's like silk and velvet and slate and fire. (*Pause*) When we play—and we're really pretty awful—but just occasionally, almost by accident, we hit it right and everyone plays *together*. Just for one bar. And it's incredible. Everyone knows they did something wonderful. It's our secret, for a moment. And then it's gone. (*Beat*) It makes you forget who you are. And it reminds you you're alive.

Silence. They listen

Alex I can hear…
Roland (*quietly*) Me too…

They listen some more, both lost in thought

Alex And I think maybe I have idea…

Roland turns to him, curious. They look at each other

Black-out

Scene 2

That night. The concert

Same configuration of seats. Roland's score on its lectern

The House Lights are up, the stage Lights dim, just picking out the

Scene 2

empty chairs. Murmur and buzz of the waiting audience. The House Lights go down and the stage Lights come up to concert state

Roland walks on stage holding his baton. He is now wearing tails and a white bow tie

The audience applaud. Roland bows nervously and gestures for silence

Roland (*in Russian*) Good evening, ladies and gentlemen. (*In English*) I'm afraid that's the full extent of my Russian. But a friend has very kindly offered to translate. (*He gestures to the wings*) Alex!

Alex strides on in a hastily improvised, ill-fitting dinner suit and bow tie

Alex (*in Russian*) Good evening, Moscow! (*He takes the applause, blinking in the bright lights, enjoying himself*)

Roland shoots him a look—Enough!

Roland You might have heard a rumour…

Alex translates into Russian

That tonight's concert was to be cancelled.

Alex translates

This was due to the unfortunate loss of our instruments.

Alex translates. But his speech is considerably longer than Roland's. It becomes obvious he's decided to tell the audience about the incident of the smuggled spliff. Interspersed with his words, he mimes the custom dog sniffing the instruments, the joint in the flute, and Roland taking the call from Mr Carmichael. Then he imitates musicians inner thoughts. It may seem like they're talking to each other but they're not. The "tone" is not dialogue but rather, interior monologue. During this they continue to "play"

Second Horn Hey, it's sounding quite good!
Cello Eh?! It's not *sounding* like anything!
Second Trumpet All I can hear is my own breath.
First Horn My fingers are sweating.
First Violin Concentrate!
Bassoon They're listening! The audience are listening!
Clarinet They can *hear* it!
Double Bass They're not walking out!
Cello Only 'cos it's sub-zero out there!
First Flute They can hear it!
Viola It's a miracle!
Oboe Shit! I made a mistake!
First Trumpet Did Roland hear it?
Oboe Oh God, he's scowling at me!
Bassoon No, he's smiling, he's encouraging us!
Timpani I've never seen him smile before, he looks insane!
Second Flute He looks lovely, he's an angel!
Second Horn I never thought this would work.
Timpani That Alex bloke's a genius!
Second Trumpet How can we thank him?
Double Bass We did a collection, weren't you there?
First Trumpet I think I was in the bogs, throwing up.
First Flute Nerves?
First Trumpet No, that black toast.
Second Horn Roland's going to get him a present tomorrow.
First Violin Concentrate everyone, it's nearly the end…
Viola Gently—remember what Roland says…
Second Flute Play each note as if it's your last…

And now we hear the last two minutes of the movement. Roland brings the piece to its slow, beautiful conclusion

The audience applaud

Roland gestures the orchestra to stand. They rise as one and bow together

Alex rushes on with a bouquet and presents it to Roland

Roland plucks a single stem and motions Second Flute forward. He presents her with the flower and she immediately swoons with the emotion of it all. Alex catches her as she falls backwards into his arms, he slaps her back to consciousness

Alex, Roland, Second Flute and the orchestra bow together one last time

Black-out

Scene 3

The following morning

Empty stage. Just the chairs

Alex wanders on in his cleaning overalls with his broom and dustpan. He comes C and looks out at the auditorium. He half raises his broom in a desultory fashion. He is in strangely low spirits

Alex (*in Russian*) Good morning, Moscow. (*He makes the vague sound of his own voice echoing in the empty auditorium*) Moscow—Moscow—Moscow… (*He shrugs and starts to slowly sweep the stage, murmuring listlessly to himself*)
>Ever since I was a young boy,
>I played the silver ball,
>From Soho down to Brighton,
>I must've played 'em all,
>But I ain't seen nothin' like him,
>In any amusement hall——

Second Flute QUIET, EVERYONE! LOOK! (*She points to the wings*)

Double Bass runs on with the real present: a brand new electric guitar

The orchestra applaud. Alex is overcome. He holds the guitar aloft and then quickly straps it on in case he's dreaming

Roland takes out his baton and with a grand gesture, like a wizard, he points to the heavens. Immediately, the Lights snap to a single spot on Alex

Roland conducts, readying the orchestra. On his cue they start to hum the opening riff of The Who's "Pinball Wizard" loud and clear—in perfect a cappella unison. Different sections of the orchestra make the sound of each instrument

And on the first big guitar chord Alex thrashes along, in full Pete Townshend whirling motion. The Lights start to come up so we can see the orchestra clearly again. And once more they're in unison. The vocal starts and their voices join in with Alex

Orchestra (*singing*) Ever since I was a young boy,
    I played the silver ball,
    From Soho down to Brighton,
    I must've played 'em all,
    But I ain't seen nothin' like him
    In any amusement hall,
    That deaf, dumb and blind kid
    Sure plays a mean pinball!

Guitar break. Alex does his stuff. When the vocals return he mimes the Pinball Wizard on his machine

    He stands like a statue,
    Becomes part of the machine,

Scene 3

> Feelin' all the bumpers,
> Always playin' clean,
> Plays by intuition,
> The digit counters fall,
> That deaf, dumb and blind kid
> Sure plays a mean pinball!
> He's a pinball wizard,
> There has to be a twist,
> A pinball wizard's got such a supple wrist.

Half the Orchestra (*in a high voice*) How do you think he does it?
The Other Half (*responding*) I don't know!
Whole Orchestra What makes him so good?

Alex continues to freak out as Roland jubilantly conducts. A final round of vocals

> Ain't got no distractions,
> Can't hear no buzzes and bells,
> Don't see no lights a-flashin'
> Plays by sense of smell,
> Always gets a replay,
> Never seen him fall,
> THAT DEAF, DUMB AND BLIND KID
> SURE PLAYS A MEAN PINBALL!

Suddenly—the whole company freeze as one. Tableau. Everyone. Still. Silent. Together

Black-out

EFFECTS PLOT

Cue 1	**Woodwind** and **Strings** start to argue **Roland**'s *mobile rings*	(Page 16)
Cue 2	As Scene 2 begins *Murmur and buzz of the waiting audience*	(Page 23)
Cue 3	**Roland**: "The Ridley Road School Orchestra!" *Applause*	(Page 24)
Cue 4	**Orchestra** mime playing *Imperceptibly bring up music; sound level to approach concert volume when* **Strings** *bring in their melody (around forty seconds)*	(Page 25)
Cue 5	After five minutes, as movement at climax *Over next twenty seconds fade music under and out*	(Page 25)
Cue 6	The music reaches its conclusion *The audience applaud*	(Page 26)